Laura Secord

Terry Barber

ACTS OF
COURAGE
SERIES

Laura Secord is published by
Grass Roots Press, a division of Literacy Services of Canada Ltd.

PHONE 1–888–303–3213
WEBSITE www.grassrootsbooks.net

ACKNOWLEDGMENTS

We acknowledge the financial support of the Government of Canada through the Book Publishing Industry Development Program (BPIDP) for our publishing activities.

We acknowledge the support of
the Alberta Foundation for the Arts
for our publishing programs.

Editor: Dr. Pat Campbell
Image research: Dr. Pat Campbell
Book design: Lara Minja, Lime Design Inc.

Library and Archives Canada Cataloguing in Publication

Barber, Terry, date
    Laura Secord / Terry Barber.

ISBN 978-1-894593-81-6

    1. Secord, Laura, 1775-1868. 2. Canada—History—War of 1812.
3. Women heroes—Canada—Biography. 4. Women pioneers—Canada—
Biography. 5. Readers for new literates. I. Title.

PE1126.N43B36458 2008   428.6'2   C2008-901989-X

Printed in Canada

Contents

Laura Secord

Laura and
the Prince

"I am a very old woman…. A few short years … will see me no more upon this earth." It is 1860. The old woman is 85. A prince reads her words. His heart goes out to the old woman.

The
Prince of Wales
becomes the King
of England in
1901.

The Prince of Wales, 1863.

Laura and the Prince

The Prince sends the old woman a gift. He sends the old woman 100 gold coins. The money will help her. The old woman is happy. The Prince believes her story. And her story is a great one. The old woman is Laura Secord.

The Prince of Wales sends the gift.

A pub in the 1800s.

Laura and James

Laura grows up in the United States. Her family moves to **Upper Canada** in 1795. Laura's father owns a pub. Laura works in the pub. James Secord spends a lot of time at the pub. James wants to marry Laura.

James Secord is born in the U.S. His family leaves the U.S. in 1776.

A store in the 1800s.

Laura and James

James and Laura marry around 1797.
By 1812, they have five children. They
own a store. They build a good life.
They are not rich, but their needs are
met. Then the war comes.

The U.S. President is James Madison.

The U.S. President declares war on Britain on June 1, 1812.

The War of 1812

Canada is ruled by Britain. The U.S. wants to take over British Canada. Canada does not want to become part of the U.S.

Britain and the U.S. go to war. The U.S. thinks the war will be short and easy to win.

Britain rules Upper Canada and **Lower Canada**.

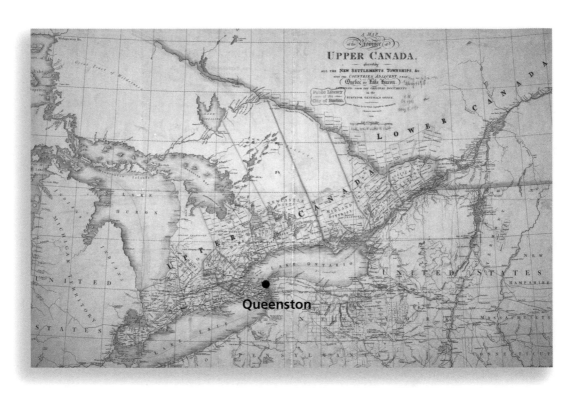

Upper and Lower Canada

The War of 1812

The war starts on June 1, 1812. The
men fight on land. The men fight at sea.
The U.S. **troops** march into Canada.
The men fight some battles in Upper
Canada. James and Laura Secord live
near the battle **zone**.

Laura
and her family
live in a village
called
Queenston.

The Battle of Queenston Heights.
October 13, 1812

The Queenston Heights Battle

The war scares Laura's five children.
The war scares Laura too. Laura does
not feel safe. It is October 13, 1812.
The U.S. troops attack Laura's village.
The battle is near her home. Laura's
family can hear the sound of gunfire.

The British win the battle at Queenston Heights.

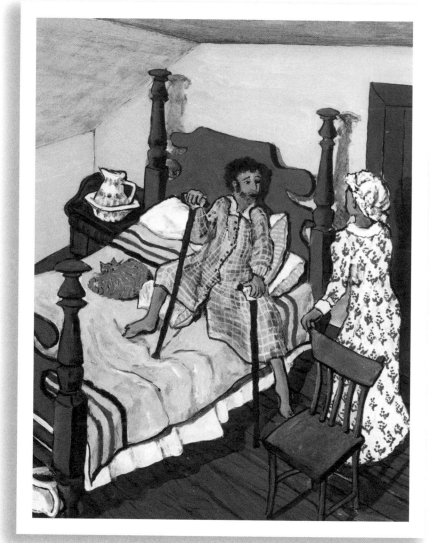

Taken from *Laura Secord: A Story of Courage* © 2001 by Janet Lunn, illustrations by Maxwell Newhouse, published by Tundra Books of Northern New York.

James hurts his leg in the battle.

The Queenston Heights Battle

James is hurt in this battle. He must rest in bed to heal. Laura acts as his nurse. With James hurt, Laura must work hard. Laura works hard to keep her family safe. Laura is a good mother.

The U.S. troops wait for their dinner.

Taken from *Laura Secord: A Story of Courage* © 2001 by Janet Lunn, illustrations by Maxwell Newhouse, published by Tundra Books of Northern New York.

The Secret Plan

U.S. troops take over the Secord
home. This often happens in war.
The troops want to be fed. Laura
makes dinner for them. The troops
drink. The troops talk too much. The
Secords learn about the troops' plan.

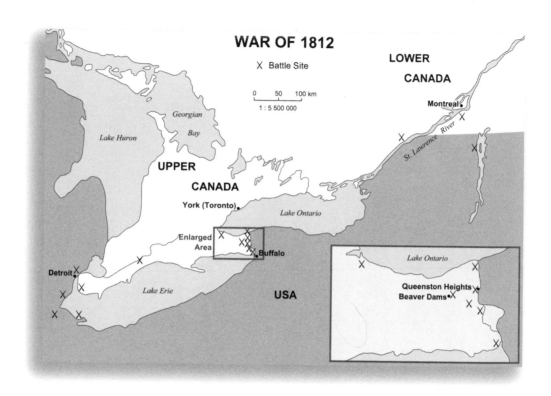

Beaver Dams

The Secret Plan

The U.S. troops plan to attack the British. The attack will take place near Beaver Dams. Over 500 U.S. troops will attack 50 British troops. The British troops will not stand a chance. If the U.S. wins, they will control Upper Canada.

Lt. James Fitzgibbon lives in this house.
Beaver Dams, Upper Canada.

Laura's Walk

Laura and James must warn the British. James is still healing. James cannot warn the British.

Laura must warn Lt. James Fitzgibbon. He is a British officer. Fitzgibbon is in charge of the troops at Beaver Dams. Laura will get her brother to help.

Lt. stands for **Lieutenant**.

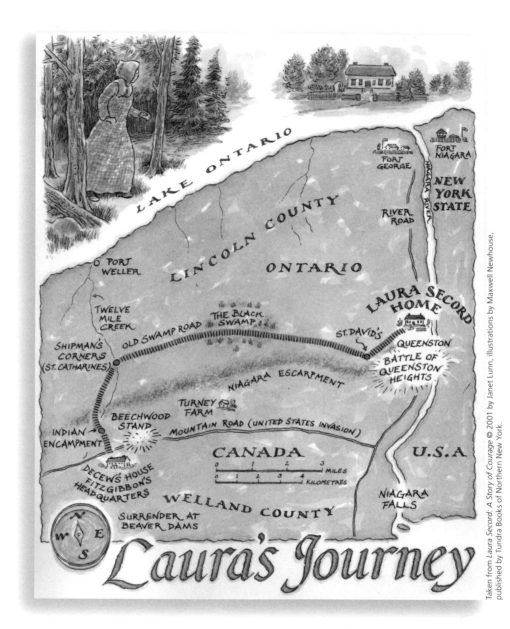

Laura's walk.

Taken from *Laura Secord: A Story of Courage* © 2001 by Janet Lunn, illustrations by Maxwell Newhouse, published by Tundra Books of Northern New York.

Laura's Walk

Laura begins her walk. She walks to her brother's house. He lives two miles away. He lives in a place called St. David's. Laura's brother cannot help. He is sick. He is too weak to walk.

Laura leaves her brother's house.

Taken from *Laura Secord: A Story of Courage* © 2001 by Janet Lunn, illustrations by Maxwell Newhouse, published by Tundra Books of Northern New York.

Laura's Walk

Laura is the only one who can warn the British. Laura must move fast. The U.S. troops plan to attack in two days. Laura must walk another 18 miles. It is a long, hard walk.

Laura starts her walk on June 22, 1813.

Laura walks through thick forest.

Laura's Walk

Laura must be careful. U.S. troops are
in the area. Laura must not be seen.
If she is seen, she will be in danger.
Laura walks through thick forest to
avoid the U.S. troops.

The creek runs through the forest.

Laura's Walk

Laura keeps walking. The day grows hotter. Laura follows a creek. She finds it easier to walk by the creek. Laura must reach Lt. Fitzgibbon as soon as she can. She keeps walking. The day gets hotter. The walk gets harder.

A mosquito hides in the shade.

Laura's Walk

Upper Canada is a wild place in
1813. Wild animals live in the forests.
Bears, wolves, and cougars live in the
forests. Mosquitoes hide in the shade.
Mosquitoes bite Laura as she walks.
She is covered with bites.

Laura Secord crosses the creek on a fallen tree.

Laura's Walk

Laura is strong. She keeps walking.
Laura is not wearing proper walking
clothes. It is hard to walk in a dress.
Her shoes have thin soles. The shoes
are not made for a 20-mile walk.
Laura's feet hurt.

The sun sets in the forest.

Laura's Walk

Laura's clothes are wet with sweat.
The sun is setting, but it is still hot.
Laura is so tired. It would feel so good
to stop and sleep. Laura will not stop.
She knows she must reach Fitzgibbon
to warn him.

The Indians take Laura to see Fitzgibbon.

Laura Meets Fitzgibbon

Laura walks on in the dark. She sees an **Indian** camp. The Indians support the British. Laura speaks to the Indians. At first, they do not believe Laura. What if she is a U.S. spy? Finally, the Indians take her to Fitzgibbon.

Laura tells Fitzgibbon about the U.S. plan.
June, 1813

Laura Meets Fitzgibbon

Fitzgibbon listens to Laura. Fitzgibbon gets Indians to help fight. The British win the battle at Beaver Dams. The British take back control of Upper Canada. By the end of 1814, the war ends. Upper Canada remains British.

The Indian warriors include the Mohawks, the Kanesatake, the Akwesasne, the Mississaugas, and the Ojibways.

A Laura Secord monument.

A Canadian Hero

Laura Secord dies in 1868. She is 93 years old. After Laura dies, more people learn about her story. Laura's act of courage changes the history of North America. Laura Secord is a Canadian hero.

James Secord dies in 1841.

Glossary

Indian: indigenous people in Canada who are not Inuit or Metis. The term First Nations has replaced the word Indian.

Lieutenant: an army or air force officer who ranks below a captain.

Lower Canada: a British colony from 1791 to 1841. It was located in present day Labrador, in the southern part of Quebec, and by the lower St. Lawrence River.

monument: a statue or building made to keep alive the memory of a person.

troop: a group of soldiers.

Upper Canada: a British colony from 1791 to 1841. It was located in present day Southern Ontario.

zone: area.

Talking About the Book

What did you learn about Laura Secord?

What words would you use to describe Laura?

What challenges did Laura face in the 1800s?

What dangers did Laura face during her
20-mile walk?

How did Laura's act of courage change history?

Picture Credits

Front cover photos (center photo): Government of Ontario Archives/621223* **(small photo):** © Library and Archives Canada, Acc. No. 1997-229-2. **Contents page (top photo):** Taken from Laura Secord: A Story of Courage © 2001 by Janet Lunn, illustrations by Maxwell Newhouse, published by Tundra Books of Northern New York; **(bottom map):** © Boston Public Library. **Page 4:** © Government of Ontario Archives/619796. **Page 6:** © HRH Albert Edward, Prince of Wales (future Edward VII) in Robes of the Garter at his wedding, 1863 (litho) (pair of 75989) Private Collection/ The Bridgeman Art Library. **Page 8:** © Library of Congress, Prints and Photographs Division, LC-USZ61-1792. **Page 10:** © The Granger Collection, New York. **Page 12:** © Library of Congress, Prints and Photographs Division, LC-USZ62-13004. **Page 14:** © Boston Public Library. **Page 16:** © Library and Archives Canada, Acc. No. 1954-153-1. **Pages 18 -20:** Taken from Laura Secord: A Story of Courage © 2001 by Janet Lunn, illustrations by Maxwell Newhouse, published by Tundra Books of Northern New York. **Page 22:** © Andreas (Andy) N Korsos, Professional Cartographer, Arcturus Consulting. **Page 24:** © C.P. Meredith/Library and Archives Canada/ PA-026914. **Page 25:** © The Granger Collection, New York. **Pages 26 - 28:** Taken from Laura Secord: A Story of Courage © 2001 by Janet Lunn, illustrations by Maxwell Newhouse, published by Tundra Books of Northern New York. **Page 30:** © istockphoto/Natalia Bratsiavsky. **Page 32:** © Government of Ontario Archives/C 127-2. **Page 34:** © istockphoto//Douglas Allen. **Page 36:** © Government of Ontario Archive/621223. **Page 38:** © istockphoto/adisa. **Page 40:** © Library and Archives Canada, Acc. No. 1996-282-10. **Page 42:** © Library and Archives Canada, Acc. No. 1997-229-2. **Page 44:** © William James Topley/Library and Archives Canada/PA-009854.

*Please note image was cropped, made into a sepia tone, and a solid tint of colour was added behind it.